Taking Care of Myself

Managing Time

By Meg Gaertner

level 2
little blue readers

www.littlebluehousebooks.com

Little Blue House is distributed by North Star Editions:
sales@northstareditions.com | 888-417-0195

Produced for Little Blue House by Red Line Editorial.

Photographs ©: Shutterstock Images, cover, 4 (top), 4 (bottom), 6–7, 11 (top), 11 (bottom), 14–15, 16 (top), 16 (bottom), 19, 24 (top left), 24 (top right), 24 (bottom left), 24 (bottom right); iStockphoto, 8, 13 (top), 13 (bottom), 20–21, 23

Library of Congress Control Number: 2021916795

ISBN
978-1-64619-495-7 (hardcover)
978-1-64619-522-0 (paperback)
978-1-64619-573-2 (ebook pdf)
978-1-64619-549-7 (hosted ebook)

Printed in the United States of America
Mankato, MN
012022

About the Author

Meg Gaertner enjoys reading, writing, dancing, and being outside. She lives in Minnesota.

Table of Contents

going to school

playing

Managing Time

People go to school.

They eat and exercise.

They play and have fun.

Managing time helps people do all of these things. People choose what to do, and they choose when to do it.

Everyday Events

Many things happen daily. It helps to do them in the same order each day. That way, you know what to expect.

For example, a boy wakes up and eats breakfast.
He brushes his teeth and goes to school.
He comes home and does homework.
Then it is time for play.

brushing teeth

doing homework

The boy eats dinner and washes the dishes.
He packs his backpack for tomorrow.
He takes a bath and brushes his teeth.
Then he goes to bed.

washing dishes

backpack

Make a plan that works
for you.
Write down the plan.
Ask an adult for help.
Then follow the plan
every day.

soccer

swimming

Special Events

Some things do not happen every day.
A girl has soccer practice on Mondays and swimming class on Fridays.

A calendar helps the girl remember these things. A calendar shows the days, weeks, and months. The girl writes down important dates.

calendar
month
July
day
2021
Monday
Tuesday
Wednesday
Thursday
Friday
Saturday
Sunday
week

Make a calendar with
your family.
You can use markers
or stickers.
Write down
important dates.

marker
MONTH
September
SUNDAY
MONDAY
TUESDAY
WEDNESDAY
THURSDAY
FRIDAY
SATURDAY

Look at the calendar every day.

That way, you know when things will happen.

You will see the fun things to look forward to.

8
9
Happy Birthday to me!
15

Glossary

backpack

markers

calendar

stickers

Index